Related

YANG WARRIORS

KAO KALIA YANG

Illustrations by
BILLY THAO

University of Minnesota Press
Minneapolis · London

Ban Vinai Refugee Camp
1986

Above the television set, in the dark room, the legendary heroes rose—the bald monk mobilizing his energy, the honorable warrior facing his enemies, the brave woman with her sword at the ready. The children sat with wide eyes and open mouths. As soon as the credits started, they raced outside to practice.

In a clearing between the houses, the children bowed to their elected leader, a ten-year-old cousin named Me, the Hmong word for *little*. Master Me was tiny. Though his arms and legs were small, his belly was round and sat on his middle like a bowl.

He had been chosen because of all the cousins in the camp, he cared the most and believed the fiercest that the children were powerful warriors. Master Me acknowledged their bows with a slow nod of his head in each direction. The children knew he would not leave any of them behind.

The children saw the enemies that existed everywhere. *The guards with their guns.* They practiced the art of throwing rocks and thrusting sticks. *The other refugee children looking for play space.* They held each other by the waist and kicked the air. *The lonely ghosts waiting on the other side of the fence.* They ran drills, running fast in one direction and then the other, so they could confuse and outsmart.

They had all heard the ghost stories: people who had died because of broken hearts or aching bellies, people who had left behind loved ones and were hungry for a return to friends and family.

There were seven boys and two girls in the group. All of them were younger than Master Me. Each morning, at the crow of the roosters, the pot-bellied boy stood at the ready, lines drawn into the dirt of the camp yard.

The children arrived one by one, each with a flat rock in hand. They went to their lines and balanced the stones on their heads. When their shadows disappeared beneath the noon sun, they ran to different homes for meager lunches of rice balls and dried fish. After lunch, they resumed their practice. The sticks in their hands were sacred swords.

The children engaged in mental battles. Master Me chose a pair of kids, and the others stood in a circle around them. The chosen ones bowed. They sat cross-legged on the dirt, eyes tightly closed, backs rigid, and sent their warrior spirits into the space between them.

The sun's heat traveled through their hair and clothing until sweat beaded their brows and dripped off their chins. The mental matches lasted from minutes to hours. The winner was the one whose concentration and stamina could not be shaken. Finally Master Me said, "Well done, disciples."

One especially hot week when camp rations were thin, Master Me took a seat, alone, in the circle of the group. He closed his eyes and meditated. After an hour, when the youngest member of the group, a five-year-old named Ong, sank on her knees from exhaustion, he opened his eyes and said, "We must leave the camp to forage for greens. The younger children need it."

The words were dangerous. Everyone knew the rule: no Hmong person could leave the camp without permission from the Thai guards. The children had

seen men and women beaten for leaving the camp. People had disappeared after reports about their leaving had been filed.

Each child drew in a breath and held it, waiting for Master Me to clarify his vision, to speak of something else, but his shoulders were stiff and his eyes far off as he explained. "There is a farmer with a pond full of morning glory nearby. If we are caught by the authorities or the adults, I will fulfill my destiny as your master. I will take all responsibility and bear the punishment."

I was a scared child, comforted by the pillow of my mother's arms, the hold of my father's hand. I was not a member of the group. My older sister Dawb was one of the two girls. She was seven years old then, a small girl with thick, messy hair, one leg shorter than the other because she had polio as a baby. Her job in the group was to carry everyone's flip-flops if they were in a fight and flee situation. She was also the best at the mental battles.

The night before the secret mission was hot and humid. A layer of dark clouds had gathered beneath a full moon. In our bed, Dawb kicked her legs restlessly.

When the songs of the crickets and the snores of our father were the only sounds in the room, Dawb whispered, "Tomorrow might be my last day."

I whispered back. "Why?"

Her voice was low and serious. "Tomorrow we are going on a mission."

I asked, "Where?"

"We are leaving the camp to look for food."

I couldn't find enough air in the room to breathe my words. "You can't."

Dawb said, "Master Me believes it is the only way to save you and the younger children. You haven't had vegetables for weeks."

I said, "I don't even like vegetables. Besides, you'll get in trouble. The guards might kill you."

She swallowed, then said, "If we don't come back tomorrow, tell Mom and Dad where we've gone. At first light, we set out."

Long after Dawb fell asleep, I could not. I listened to the sound of mice scurrying, watched the light of the moon through the slits in the walls.

The next morning when I woke, the bed was empty. My mother had left to tend her small garden of cilantro and green onions. My father was out carrying the day's water from the well. I looked at my sister's place beside me and I knew she was not in the yard, standing at her line. I put my hands over my quivering belly.

I watched the adults prepare lunch. My father blew into the red embers of last night's fire until a small flame danced among the burnt wood. My mother smashed chilis, her green onion, cilantro, and salt in the mortar and pestle. They were thin, their faces tired. I knew they were probably hungry and scared, too. Each time I closed my eyes, I saw the end of the battle scenes from the historical Chinese dramas my sister and our cousins loved: smoke rising from fallen houses, the bodies of the horses, men, women, and children scattered across the dirt road, bleeding and still. Fallen flags trampled into wet dirt.

What if my sister were killed? I was about to tell my mother about the secret mission when I saw Ong. She was wet, and she carried a plastic bag of greens. She leaned it quietly by the doorway. Before anyone noticed, she left.

I followed.

> "Ong, where's Dawb?"
> "Hurt."

I blinked the tears away.

> "What happened?"
> "Many were injured."

The two of us ran behind the corn husk shack. My heart pounded with each step.

I saw my sister lying on the dusty earth, her head on Master Me's lap. There was a wound on the side of her forehead. Blood ran down her face. Another cousin was also on the ground. His foot was wrapped in an old shirt.

Ong yelled, "Grandma's coming!"

The children scrambled.

By the time Grandma arrived with the switch in her hand, her head shaking left and right, the line of her mouth tight, only the fallen ones remained, with Master Me now on his knees.

Most of the group had been caught when they scattered. There was not much talk—no one wanted to attract the attention of the guards. Grandma's switch flew into butts; whimpers and yelps were caught in throats. Master Me suffered the worst of the consequences. Grandma said, "You are the oldest. You could have killed them all. If the authorities find out ... what would happen?"

For lunch that day, the younger children and I ate fresh morning glory. The greens were fried with garlic oil and seasoned with fish sauce. I can still hear the crunch of the stalks and taste how the oil made the rice slippery, how the garlic made all of it slightly sweet. None of the children in the group chose to enjoy the meal with us. They watched us clear our plates. It was our first taste of freedom.

Before lunch the group had been naughty children, playing a game, but after that meal all of us saw that they were brave and powerful.

I knew the adults had all survived a war, but I had
never imagined we children could be warriors.
Long before we left Ban Vinai Refugee Camp,

the Yang Warriors showed us what existed beyond
the fence and gave us the courage we needed

I see them now, far away from that dry, dusty, hungry place we shared beneath the burning sun, the group of warriors standing strong. Master Me, firm belly forward. Ong on her tiptoes, trying to be older than her years. Dawb, chin held high, her stronger leg braced against the earth. They were my heroes, not the characters in the movies, and they are glorious in the sun of my youth.

AUTHOR'S NOTE

The Yang family before leaving Ban Vinai Refugee Camp for the United States.

LONG BEFORE I knew what superheroes were, I fell in love with the Yang Warriors. They were my sister and my cousins—each standing in their line in the hot sun, faces trickling with sweat, eyes closed fiercely or opened wide and unblinking. In Ban Vinai Refugee Camp, they trained for a day when their skills would save us all. Under the hot sun, they showed me that the most important work in the world is the work we give ourselves; the most important roles we'll have in life are the ones we assign ourselves. In that place where I was a child with little to do, hiding in the shade of tall trees and the safety of my mother's and my father's arms, the Yang Warriors ran with purpose, fought against ideas of safety, and risked everything for something better.

Now, over thirty years later, I look back to that blinding little world that was our life: above and beyond the fence, the shadows of the men and women looking out, I see the young warriors bravely looking in, looking at each other, looking for the places and future we couldn't imagine. These warriors first taught me all the skills I would need to become a writer: spirit, purpose, conviction, and daring. They taught me how to live without fear.

Even more, they taught me how to have fun with others, how to go on adventures with those who love us, and how to salvage from our experiences not only the things we needed to survive but also the hope and beauty of sharing life's responsibilities. I hope the Yang Warriors can do the same for each and every one of you.

ILLUSTRATOR'S NOTE

I AM a Hmong American who was born and raised in Minnesota. I never witnessed a horrendous war, lived in a refugee camp, or had to leave my family behind. All the stories I have heard were told by my family and survivors, and all their experiences can be traced back to the oldest art form within Hmong culture: Paj Ntaub, pronounced pa ndau. Paj Ntaub is a traditional Hmong textile art that requires intensive labor of various techniques combined with embroidery to communicate stories and motifs of the Hmong experience. As an adult, looking at works of Paj Ntaub with mature eyes, I am attracted not just to its artistry but also to the ancestors who were brave and resilient in continuing the journey of the Hmong people.

Through my intensive research for these illustrations I learned that within Hmong art (and language) a puzzle of messages and truths remains that is waiting to be unfolded. To illustrate this book to the core of truth, I had to discover the hidden treasure. I studied Hmong culture and traveled back into the history of the Hmong—and I found resilience, compassion, and hope.

We can agree on one thing: life is not easy. But through a child's eye, life is fun. If children's books, including this one, have taught me anything as an illustrator, they have taught me this: to wake up early in the morning, see the orange sky hidden behind the horizon of a purple hill, and smile, because life is beautiful and worth fighting for.

Ban Vinai Refugee Camp. Photograph by Doug Hulcher, copyright minorsasia.org.